Holy Oil

for the House of God

poems by
Faith Forster

PUSH
PUBLISHING

ICHTHUS
CHRISTIAN FELLOWSHIP

First published in 2012 by PUSH Publishing

www.pushpublishing.co.uk

A catalogue record for this book is
available from the British Library

ISBN-13:   978-0-9553783-7-9

Cover design and typesetting by Joseph Laycock
Cover photo by Rob George
Illustrations by Walter Hayn

MIX
Paper from
responsible sources
FSC   FSC® C013056
www.fsc.org

Printed and bound in Great Britain by
TJ International Ltd, Padstow, Cornwall

Contents

Dedication

To Roger, the inspiration of my life,
and to the rest of my family who are a constant joy
and support, and a great encouragement to pray!

Also to my wider family of the church,
without whom this book would not have been written.

Foreword

This varied collection demonstrates not only a poet's skill with language, but a deep empathy for people in our joys and sorrows.

There is much here that is psalm-like, a practical and rooted kind of poetry crafted on the front lines of life in its beauty, rawness and messy-ness, poetry that is not so much made as uncovered in the pursuit of a much greater quest, to know God and his mysterious ways.

Graham Kendrick

Makeway Music
June 2012

Acknowledgement

My grateful thanks to Sarah Fordham who was
a constant encouragement and help in this process,
and to Paula Payne and Anna Raisey
for typing up the poems.

A very big thank you also to Walter Hayn
who despite the time pressure produced
some lovley line drawings to illustrate the poems,
and to patient Joe Laycock for drawing the
whole thing together in record time.

Preface

Some people who have experienced my ministry primarily in its teaching/preaching/pastoral forms, may be surprised to learn that I also write poetry. Others will not be surprised, having urged me to publish for years! Many of my poems lend themselves to reading in the context of church meetings and celebrations. Some have even had dance and movement included in the performance. To have a full inventory of 'performance poems' may therefore be useful.

Other poems were written on pastoral occasions, such as infant dedications, weddings and funerals. They were written to sum up my thoughts and prayers, and were sometimes read out loud at the appropriate event. Where names are included in the text of the poem, they can be substituted if the poem is applicable to someone else's situation. I think they help us think more deeply about life and death, or about the potential for a new infant life. They were written with much love and prayer for the subjects of the verse.

In selecting the poems I wanted to include here, I have laid aside many that I enjoyed writing, but which don't quite fit here: for example, poems written to my family members, which are full of love but which seem too personal to publish here, and 'stream of consciousness' poems that are of limited value to others.

I believe poetry is part of my prophetic gift, and has found most expression in my preaching and pastoral ministry. Words are beautiful, powerful things, and I love to use them to explore the only true Word.

Faith Forster
June 2012

Section

Performance Poems

1

i. Advent

Rumour of Angels

'Oh, my friend, you can write them off,
they are dead to the world
like those who dream,
they have seen a vision of angels …'

Zachariah in the temple
laid the burden of his crying
– the people without a vision and dying –
unspeakable joy possessed his heart,
his eyes were opened,
as one set apart
he saw the angel of the Lord …
(though John would be
a man of the wilderness,
hard as steel
that is forged as a sword,
yet the promise of his coming brought joy and gladness,
beautiful the speaking of that word …)

Mary is lost to the world, past shame,
steadfast in heart since the angel came,
rejoicing in spirit and
seeing through tears
not the cross that stands in the midst of the years
to pierce her soul,
but the joy that springs from an empty tomb,
and the healing that makes us whole …

The shepherds were safe in the womb of night,
till it all began – the pressure, relentless
bands constricting, moulding their humanity …
worlds then heaving, breaking open,
they were born precipitately
into light …

ears assailed with voices – thunder
short with lightning
filled the brain …
(is this life and joy or only pain …?)
now, the darkness once more round them,
beatific vision gone,
can they ever live again in night?
humans, once their eyes are opened,
grow addicted to the light …

You, whose ears have never heard
living words that leave you dumb,
you, whose eyes have never seen
beauty that can make you numb
to all this tawdry world …
tell me, do you pity them, or envy …?

Hope

Hurtling through untold dimensions He came
the shock-waves before Him
attacking earth's sin
assailing the barriers with rhythmic assault
till defences are breached
and the heavens pour in,
He has come ...

and in a cradle lies
the very sun and centre of another world
launched from its heavenly orbit
on a predetermined journey to the earth ...

and all that beauteous world
streamed in His wake
as stars and angels danced for joy before Him
lighting His progress through the watchful skies ...
while on beleaguered earth,
the evil flood was rising
and the darkness crept upon us
and the stranglehold was even at our neck ...

But hear the cry of joy!
The Lord has given us a sign
a virgin has conceived and borne
a baby boy ...
What darkness can withstand
that holy coming?
What power of death or hell could mar
His radiant hour?

This is the stone
– hewn by no human hand
– that fell
into our midst with devastating power
to shatter sin and grow and fill the earth ...
Welcome, Immanuel! ...

Shadows

I do not want to walk in shadowland
where doubts and fears and nameless ugly things
creep slithering from recesses of the mind,
to lurk in corners or the bend of stairs
and cast their darkening shades about my head
in my lone climbing …

I want to be like Mary when the Spirit came …
who knew the beat of wings above her,
the shadow of the Most High falling
softly
like a cloak about her …
stirrings deep within her and
a breath upon her face, like some
sweet zephyr from another world
where holy things are born …
where life springs out of barrenness,
no shade of doubt can linger
and where nothing is impossible
with God …

Of Course She Dreamed

Of course she dreamed
on winter nights
when wind blew thinly
flickering candle flame ...
she spun her webs of joy
about His name,
swirling the silk of bridal veil and gown
against her face
(strong features
gentled by intelligence and grace)
herself a cloud adrift on rosy skies
up to the tranquil height that flies
then hazily
        crazily
                falling in joy
the world beneath her feet a bed of down
to cradle her
and gently warm
her new-born boy ...

The angel woke her briskly from that dream
into a world where sharper colder air
blows keenly through the mind
to pierce the soul ...
two hands gripped hers, a voice, 'Talitha koum!' ...

Fully awake at last
she shook the cobwebs from her brain
and in the light of day
she saw
the pain, the shame, the poverty, the fear,
the loneliness, the exile,

nails and spear,
and over all the outstretched hands of God …

and quietly she rose,
folded and put away her dreams
like bedclothes …

For what do dreams matter
when the day has come
and God calls you and offers you His hand …?

The Door

Open the door … some wonder lies within,
Tread softly, not to break the holy spell
that grips the earth this night,
freezing the world in its headlong flight,
its reckless-flinging, feckless-winging flight
through hell-born sin
to man-made hell …
Some life-force is at work – we feel its power
stirring the deadened heart, till like a flower
its tight-curled bud unfurls, and gropes for light …

The wise of men are drawn upon a quest,
led by a star;
the others simply dazzled where they are,
pierced by a light, a vision, something far,
remote, earth-shaking, has drawn near …
they, frozen first in fear,
are strangely warmed and comforted, sent forth
to seek now with the wise what all desire …

And here this door, this stable door that hides
the object of our quest – the eternal fire,
the flame that keeps the universe in motion,
the heartspring of all worlds, the core of being –
this we would see and worship in our seeing …
… Open the door, tread gently, step inside,
we seek a King who calls for our devotion …

A quiet mother lifts a weary head,
pauses a moment, knowing what we seek,
then, brushing back the straw that cloaks his bed,
she strokes her baby's cheek …

And He in splendour lay
– the Maker of the universe –
among the hay,
and in that tiny form we saw the power
that could alone redeem us in our darkest hour …

The turning of the tide
Lay in that mortal body, frail and small
- a tide that reached its zenith when He died,
broken and bleeding, run through, crucified,
yet being turned, could wash us back to shore …

All this we saw and more,
and wept and laughed for joy, kneeling before that stall …
O come let us adore Him now,
the Lord of all …

The Tree

The room lay still and silent, only
the sweet high tinkling music of
innumerable fragile spheres
rang out their joyful message
from the tree ...
which winked and glowed in radiancy
its branches heavy with the weight of light
and deeper gift-wrapped burdens in its heart ...

And one small child
crept softly into the darkened room
to stand apart
and gaze in silence at the sight,
speechless in awe and wonder at this alien tree
that fruited light and splendid mystery ...

As long ago
another child
first opened wide His eyes in gloom
and saw a light no other eyes could see,
He also was transfixed in heart
long long before His body knew
that rooting to the ground ...

The Word was silent then
as down the years
the distant hidden music reached
His infant ears,
and by the shining of His natal star
in that dim corner of the world's own night
He saw a tree all radiant with light,
its dark, moist branches glistening from afar,
and He Himself the red-wrapped gift
that hung there heavily ...

Yet on that still and holy night
when first He looked upon the sight
He did not turn his face away
from his own Christmas tree,
that waited
for His gift to you and me ...

Immanuel

He made himself a cloak of our humanity
and wore it as no man has ever done
it fitted him ...
On us it hangs in limp folds, creasing where
we are not large enough to fill its huge capacity
Yet oddly straining here and there
in tense, taut ugly patches where
we suffer from obesity
we should be small and humble, yet are not ...
we are mis-shapen pitiable things
But he within the manger laid
was beautifully made ...

His eyes were eyes that saw all and forgave all
His ears caught words that mouths could never voice,
the faint, despairing heart-call
His smile – sun rippling tranquil seas – sang out 'Rejoice!'
His hands outstretched made contact, strong to heal and soothe
His mouth dripped truth like honey on our head
yet sharp as any scalpel cutting deep
drew tears with words no other could have said ...

His feet, how beautiful upon the hills
the dust, the callouses, the blood,
of feet that worked, that walked this stony earth
through fire and flood
to bring good news
– the lowly feet of one who came to serve ...

His heart that pumped not human blood alone
eight pints of living fluid to His flesh and bone
but by some secret alchemy
gave love beside,

pulsating through His human frame
to warm all dying things in range
when that did not suffice
it willed to flood the world with life
and found an outlet through a spear-hole in His side ...

What form He wore
when human life He bore!
O Son of Man, humanity became you,
to you it was no fetter,
help us who wear it too, to wear it better

The Gift

He clothed Himself in wrappings we could recognise
warm flesh and hair and hands and loving eyes
the eternal Spirit hidden in our human clay
and given to us
with love from God
on Christmas day ...

And we unwrapped Him roughly, carelessly
tearing His flesh and plucking at His beard
our unbelief and cruelty and shame
so painfully revealed
as we laid bare
that gift which lay beyond our power to grasp ...

But as the wrappings fell away
His pure bright spirit flamed out deathlessly
breathlessly
we caught a glimpse of His glory
– briefly unconfined that shining
through the mantle of our night ...

Now hid once more from sight
not in the stuff of earth but in the cloudy skies
He waits that second-time unveiling,
heavens torn apart and yielding
unrelenting glory to our eyes ...

And in that moment,
dazed as shepherds
dumb as any startled priest,
when words have ceased
love still will pour
from hearts and lives our thanks
for such a gift ...

Humiliation

'A little lower than the angels'
seems a little wide of the mark
when you think of that cattle-shed
and Him
too empty of self to know the meaning of humiliation,
smiling serenely with straw about His head ...

and I wonder ...
Would they ever have found
that small bright living star
if they hadn't been led?
They who were counted wise among men
would they ever have stooped so low as that manger-bed?

It is a problem not resolved
though centuries have rolled,
for still we hear Him
(selfless as ever)
invite us to share His throne
and,
eager to ascend the height
to reign with Him,
we seek a way
but cannot seem to find the place to start ...

The angels laugh with pure delight
while He
with understanding heart
smiles and points down there among the hay ...

Light in our Darkness

A dark and silent hillside, bathed in sleep.
A few rough-spoken peasants, guarding sheep …
To these there came that dazzling, fearful light,
Piercing the shrouding blackness of the night;
And mortal ears received that angel song,
Steel-sharp, wine-sweet, ice-clear, fire-pure, death-strong.

Men warred, slaves groaned, and earth with violence rang,
Yet 'Peace on earth', the joyful chorus sang,
'Goodwill to men' the heavenly message ran,
(While Herod planned to kill each new born man),
'Good news we bring' – to all by sorrow torn,
'This day the Saviour of the world is born!'

Jesus, whose voice could bid the tumult cease,
Come to our troubled hearts and bring release!
O Everlasting Father, Prince of Peace …

Mary, rejoice!

The life was planted in her as a seed
– not, indeed,
without her will
for in the still, quiet watches of the night,
the promise came, which, having heard,
she welcomed,
'let it be to me according to your word' …

From this transaction grew that life,
she nurtured it within her
bore its shame
and suffered pain
to bring the Christ-child forth at last with joy
she fed him, clothed him, guarded him and when
dark hearts and evil hands groped for the boy,
she fled with him where they could not destroy
the growing life …

At length her sorrows, anxious care and pain
had their reward indeed
for in her need
and ours
that very life which she had brought to birth
fell like a seed into its native earth
and sprang up multiplied …

Mary, rejoice, your tears were not in vain,
the life you bore within you was your Saviour

And we who daily bear the life of God
within us, tending and guarding it, perhaps with tears,
have too this hope that in the coming years
He shall be manifest in us, the Christ, our Saviour

Break-through

You are the God of breaking-through
slashing earth's protective shroud
pouring heaven through the cloud
stunning
        shepherds
                touched by You …

You are He who smote the skies
with the light your hand had made
wise men magnetised
obeyed,
   – starlight
        spilling
                from their eyes …

You are a Sign, the sword You wield
pierces every
hidden part
that the thoughts of many hearts
        good or ill
            might be revealed …

You are the God of breaking-through
– break the bonds that hold us fast!
Purify our souls at last
till we worship
        only
          You …

Star of Wonder

O star that guided them aright
who sought the Christ-child wandering
will you not guide us through the night
of earth's lone seeking?
Encompassed by your radiant light
who would not sing?

For you will always lead to Him
in whom we live and breathe and move
and He is joy unspeakable
Whose name is Love ...
What though there be some pain to bear
some loss sustained
along the way?
The riches that in Him are gained
Fade not away ...

The Song of the Magi

Oh it was beautiful, who would deny it?
Don't be amazed that we travelled so far,
We were mere mortals, no match for the beauty
that pierced us and drew us to follow that star …

Light like a river poured endlessly on us,
in us, around us, it banished the night,
drinking it deep we were men in a stupor
heady and drunk with that radiant light …

Herald of morning conceived in the midnight
deep in the heavens they witnessed its birth
rising at dayspring to conquer with beauty
in unequal combat the strong of the earth …

Oh we were happy, don't waste on us pity …
weeping and laughing we danced on our way
feet torn and bleeding still flew on their mission
lightly we trod at the end of the day …

Love was upon us within us around us
joy like a blessing anointed our head
dancing we came to that Bethlehem stable,
stricken we fell on our face as men dead …

Bright shone the herald to welcome His coming
star of the morning to conquer the night
but pale grows the starlight when dawn is arising,
strong is the sun in the strength of its might …

Dayspring had risen on wings that bring healing,
life-giving rays poured His love on the earth
Bright shone His face as the sun in its splendour,
Oh we were blessed to be there at His birth!

Gift of a Wise Man

I would have brought Him gold
The gold of faithful service, finely wrought
The honours of a battle bravely fought –
But I have failed
And stumbled under pressures that assailed
I cannot bring to Him the prize I sought.

I would have brought Him incense
The frankincense that speaks of heavenly things
The fragrance of a life that prays and sings
Through every trial
But there is little incense in my vial
I have no store of holy offerings.

No gold, no frankincense
Are mine to lay before Him at His shrine
Only a heart brimful of myrrh is mine –
That deathly spice
That lingers round a lonely sacrifice
Or mingles in some bitter cup of wine.

For You, my holy king,
I only have a gift of myrrh to bring
A life made up of many a bitter thing
But will you take
The trials, the tribulations for your sake
And count them as my loving offering?

The God-man

He slipped into the stream of time,
the stream of human history
embracing anonymity
and veiling His divinity
that He might be a servant to us all ...

And we could hold our head with pride
because the god-man glorified humanity
by coming thus,
by thus becoming one of us
He purged from us the shame of Adam's fall ...

Not that He came to give to us
a glory not our due
(as if to watch the god-man live
were but to see what man could do,
the perfect heights he could attain!)

Not in some long-awaited vindication
of humankind there lies the inspiration
but in the revelation
of God himself,
The Father seen in Jesus Christ the Son,
who was ...

the   lowly
one,   the
holy   one,
the   healer
the   friend
the   master,   the   teacher
the   servant,   the   preacher
the   beginning   and   the   end
the   workman
the   shepherd
the   lion,
the   lamb
the   lonely
one,   the
only   one
— I AM ...

Truly the glory of God was seen
in the face of Jesus Christ His Son
and we beheld His glory, full of grace and truth ...

ii. Easter & Pentecost

Cry of Dereliction

'Why have you left me, God?' He cried
and the heavens darkened in reply,
the thunder rolled and the firm earth shook
while the people, trembling, turned to look
as the cry of Jesus tore the air,
when He tasted our despair ...

And the sorrows and heartache of all the world
were held in that bitter and searching word,
'Why have you left me, God?'

But the pall of darkness did not lift,
no ray of sunlight brought a rift
in the cloud of horror that cloaked the earth
as they murdered the only man of worth
Oh God, this world has seen too well
the terrible blackness of hell ...

Then, Jesus, they watched as you bowed your meek head,
and every ear hung on the words that you said,
'Father, now into your loving hands
I commit myself, for you understand ...'

And you knew no more of the earthquake's shock,
for your heart had found the rock

Glimpses

Horror …
       darkness …
              grief and tears …
All the hatred of the years
against You, my God,
vent in blood

Jesus …
       Saviour …
              Lord and King …
Sum of every lovely thing,
broken and bruised,
rejected, misused …

I …
       a sinner …
              lone and lost …
Sought and bought at utmost cost,
loved of God
loved unto blood

For Real

Not in some vaguely mystic sphere
did Christ live here
but as a human child,
full-blooded, laughing, loving youth
yet undefiled ...
and when He grew to man
He broke the ancient curse of sin
not in some vaguely mystic way
but when sharp thorns had crowned His head
and when His human blood was shed
and when He rose up from the dead
that glorious day ...
Not vague but certain is our hope in Him ...

A Vision

I looked into the heart of God,
And there I saw a cross;
No other thing, nought else beside,
Just Love embracing Loss;
I wondered and I marvelled there,
I wept, adored, and cried in prayer,
'Is this a heart that I can wear?
Can I Your nature share?'

I gazed and gazed into that heart,
And worshipped what I saw,
The God Whose heart enfolds a cross
Prostrated me with awe;
'My God, can Your love really be
A love that chooses Calvary,
And bears its cross eternally?
– Then give that love to me!'

Resurrection

I watch the flowers blossom and the earth begin to bud,
as winter fades away before the spring;
I hear the rivers chatter as they wash away the mud,
and all around the birds begin to sing;
I see the face of nature and I read a message there
as every year she glories in the spring,
I love to feel the surging hope pulsating in the air
as life begins to stir in everything:

    Yet deep within
I know these things
are but a faint reflection,
They say to me
that there will be
a greater resurrection …

I see the perfect beauty of a tiny new-born child,
the innocence and purity of youth,
the noble aspirations of a young man unbeguiled,
with all his earnest strivings after truth;
And then I watch the years that take the freshness from his brow,
and dull the cutting-edge of youth's desire,
the high ideals have given way to realism now,
and sin and sorrow dampened manhood's fire:

    But still I hear a whisper
    in the midst of my dejection
'Look unto Me
and you will see
true manhood's resurrection.'

I sorrow at the graveside of a loved one or a friend,
and think how brief and shadowy life seems,
we weep and struggle, laugh and love until our journey's end,
then we must leave to others all our dreams.
Were they in vain, the hopes, the fears, the inward battles fought,
the precious store of wisdom, hard-acquired?
Do all life's longings end in death, without the goal they sought?
Or shall we see the fruit of our desire?

Then firm and clear, a Voice I hear
That ends my introspection,

    'Have faith in Me
    for you will see
    all lovely things
    restored in Me.
    Do you believe?
    Can you not see
    the secret of eternity?
    – I am the Resurrection.'

The Bride

The Spirit leads my thoughts back to the Cross
And bids me look once more on Calvary
Beyond familiar truths I see a mist
What is it Lord, that you would show to me?

I see my Saviour hanging on the Tree
I know that to atone for sin He died
But now the mist unfolds and I see too
He suffered that we might be sanctified ...

What mystery unsearchable is here!
The Bridegroom dies that He might win His bride
As Adam lay in silent deathly sleep
That Eve might be created from His side

This was the deepest longing of His heart
To see His Church presented as His Bride
No spot, no stain, to mar Her lovely face
Her radiant glory shining at His side

This was the vision bright before His eyes
As Christ endured the bitter agony
His bride, His Body, cleansed, united, pure
Exalted with Him for eternity

Not Alone

'He was alone ...' I hear you whisper softly,
'all alone ...
in that dark hour when in Gethsemane
He faced His destiny ...
and you will be alone, yes, all alone ...
down through the darkening valley of the years,
who knows what there awaits you?
– maybe tears
and pain and sorrow, loneliness and loss,
or maybe just the slowly crushing burden
of a daily cross ...
How will you face it, since you are alone ...
Yes all alone, poor child, you are alone ...'

Ah, subtle foe!
The whisper falling softly on my ear
Whilst in the sentient tissues of my heart,
you thrust your poisoned dart ...
But all in vain, you cannot harm me so,
For though you speak the truth it is in part ...

– The One who said
that He was left alone when friends forsook Him
said also that He yet was not alone
for God was with Him ...
You thrust your darts in vain, my enemy,
for He has said that very thing to me,
And I am not alone ...

Living Water

... Hot sun
scorched baked earth, dust clung
feet burned, head swam,
parched tongue could mouth but one
cracked, gasping word,
'water!' ...

... He waited and she came
(the well was near,
she'd drunk before
and often
but still the same
deep craving thirst
brought her for more ...)

Laboriously
she drew the water
(never mind that man who stares
– so he looks thirsty
aren't we all?
why, all the world is thirsty, so
who cares? ...)

... Now for the drink,
delicious soaking
sinking coolness,
soothing aching throat
and swollen tongue
(if only this would quench that craving
once for all ...)

'Give me a drink ...'
(He spoke!
he can't be asking me,

why surely any fool can see
I'm thirsty too ...
my need is such
there's not enough
for him and me ...)

'Daughter ...' (he said)
'If you but knew
the gift of God,
and who it is who speaks to you,
you'd ask of Me and I would give you
water ...
– living water, springing, rushing,
rivers deep within you gushing,
wells of water in the heart,
saturating every part ...
you need never thirst again
never die for want of rain
never see the thirsty die
while you stand helpless by ...
will you believe?
can you receive
from Me?'

She came,
a dried up withered soul,
an empty hole,
she went away refreshed, renewed,
– fountains of living water spewed
their goodness to the world ...
God poured His life out to her
so that through her
others need not ever thirst
nor die ...

She came – and so may I ...

Water and Spirit

He broke the waters at His birth
while angels sang and all the skies
resounded with His high renown ...

Then when the years were fully ripe
He broke through water once again
and, glittering, shining, waited
His baptismal crown ...

And heaven, having held its breath,
released it in a burst of power
and in a flash of silver wings
the dove of God flew down
a streak of joyful energy
that swooped and dipped and soared
on shining rays of glory winging,
soft and low His love-voice singing,
'Glory, glory, glory to the Lord ...'

And those who watched and wondered, saw
the mesh of flesh and spirit there
the wedding of the human and divine ...
– and from that spirit union
the power was birthed
that set men free,
that healed the lame, released the dumb
made blind eyes see ...

Now in her flesh, new-washed and clean,
in meekness and humility
His church awaits His promise of her bridal hour
– that union with the Holy One that brings to birth
the glory and the power ...

iii. Life with God

Listening

Lord make my ear
Like the ear of a child
Open and clear,
Pure, undefiled
Help me to listen
As one set apart
Leaning upon you
To hear from your heart

Your voice is to me
like the waters in flood
Lord, touch my ear
with the oil and the blood
Yours is the wisdom
That I draw upon
Sing in my spirit
Your beautiful song

You are the shepherd
Your sheep hear your voice
I hear you now and I rejoice

Words of Life

O precious, precious Word of God!
You are to thirsty souls more dear
than rain is to the barren earth
or music to a jaded ear ...
You are more beautiful by far
than all that people praise as Art
You are the bright and morning star
whose glory captivates my heart ...

You are my rock, my resting place
when all around is war and strife,
I fly into your sweet embrace
to read the words of love and life ...
O precious Word, could I but stay
here at your feet from day to day,
my soul, made pure, would scare decay
nor would sin steal my joy away ...

The Vine

(written for Dilys, my long-time prayer partner who
went to heaven, still praying, in April 2005)

Rooted in the secret place
no-one knows how deep it goes
drawing on the hidden springs
shaded from the burning rays
quietly it grows …

knowing that in coming days
barren branch will turn to green
buds of faith and hope will grow
into clustered promises –
fruit that can be seen …

Holy Oil

Love, ah love can rain in torrents,
swelling rivers in the heart,
surging chasing pulsing racing,
urging on till all encasing
breaks – and sweetly self-effacing
love floods forth to play her part.

So it was when Mary softly,
trembling more with joy than fear,
took the jar that held her treasure
(costlier far than she could measure)
in her hands and, taut with pleasure,
bent on giving, ventured near.

Jesus sat apart, expectant,
wrapped in stillness, heavenly Dove;
Mary, all her heart a roaring
flaming furnace, knelt adoring
till from her clasped hands came pouring
ointment sweet to anoint her love.

Priceless fragrance, poured on Jesus,
precious worship none could mar,
costlier still the hands that crushing
with the strength of love's uprushing
brought that fragrant ointment gushing
from its softly-shattered jar.

Lord, we come like Mary bringing
our most precious offering;
fire the hearts which thus adore you,
strengthen hands that break before you
love's own treasured gift
and pour you
holy oil to anoint you King

Holy to the Lord

What a glacial world we have made of His holiness,
remote and inaccessible as that far pole
whose unrelenting whiteness chills the soul
and numbs the senses …
where man who clings and strives with iron will
finds at the last he is an alien still,
and in some lonely spot the strongest fall
and leave no mark – snow swiftly covers all …

so why did God (who should have understood
how we would view such things)
choose for His model of the ultimate good
– Aaron … ?

He comes, he stuns the senses
blows the mind,
he wears
unutterable beauty as a breastplate
stones of fire
assail the eyes
their flashes starting-pistols for the pulses …
ears are pierced exquisitely –
bells, bells,
ringing rapier-like but sweet …
And oh the fruit! Mouth watering luscious
pomegranates dripping juice
and tantalising visions of another Eden
(not lost this time but won) …

And tell me now, what human artistry
(for artists have a care for reputation)
would run amok with colours, blatant, bold,
then wrap the whole sense-stealing show in brightest gold
without restraint?
And who would dare
(breathe gently if you can)
to place such startling beauty on a mortal man,
then fasten to his forehead with a golden cord
that stunning message –
    'HOLY TO THE LORD' ... ?

Hour of Need

He brings good news
to those who stagger
burdened
yoked to works of sin,
be free! He says and, touching, heals
the pressure sores within ...

He sings good news
to those whom sorrow,
drowning,
threatens to destroy,
the oil on troubled waters is
the kingly oil of joy ...

He breathes good news
on those who see
their dreams to hopeless ashes turn,
his laser beauty shining
kindles
hope that brightly burns ...

He is good news
when, blind
        imprisoned
chained by every evil power,
his spirit rising Samson-like
makes faith the victor
in that hour ...

Oh love that sees
the damaged reed,
which men would careless
cast aside,
and heals it in the hour of need,
be glorified ...
            be glorified ...

Sing to the Light

Dawn
       breaks
            slowly silently
imperceptibly turning to grey …
      shadows stir
        and stumble off grumbling
night is dissolving and draining away,
        soon comes the day …

Now it is time, it is time to wake up!
Cast off the soul-numbing blanket of night;
treasures once hidden in darkness are waiting,
Rise and be ready
    to welcome the light!

Light
       bright
           sweetness is shining
probing and searching with heart-warming rays
       stirring the deadness
       with fiery fingers
softening harshness with blood-tinged haze,
        Beautiful day …

This is the Light that will never be vanquished
Sing to Him now, let your song reach the skies!
Herald the dawn and rejoice in its brightness
Jesus the Dayspring has come,
      so arise,
          sing to the Light …!

The Battle

(You have not yet resisted unto blood, striving against sin
Hebrews 12:4)

The hosts of darkness seem arrayed
about my head,
and I would be dismayed
had You not said
that You are with me till the end of time ...
If I must die
I'd rather die in battle
than in the coward's cell ...
I cannot watch the people herd
like cattle
into the mouth of hell,
and leave the powers of darkness unassailled ...

If battle there must be
then I must fight
nor will I look for
victory
in just one night
(I do not underestimate the foe) ...
But shall I give to Him what costs me nought
and call it sacrifice?
If I with His own life-blood have been bought
shall I pay less a price
in bringing others into liberty?

The Cross is still a cross
that causes pain,
it seems
there always must be loss
before a gain

(This is a rule that every soldier knows)
If in the Master's footsteps I would tread,
the path is known ...
He was not made a victor till He shed
blood of His own ...
Nor will the victory come to me another way ...

Love's rest

O love that fills eternity
come now and reign in me,
that guided by your faithful rod
I may be free ...

For You have walked this earth and know
the bondage of its day
You know too well the clinging power
of human clay ...

O free me from the things of sense
the passing things of time
that I may taste love's deathlessness
its power sublime ...

For darkness and the mind's despair
are banished by Your face
and in Your love my heart has found
its resting place ...

The Cries of the Lost

I saw them living, yes,
But just to die – no light, no hope,
To spur them to a higher plane
Than this;
The land itself was desolate
A desert that was mirrored
In their eyes.

I saw them lying down
To sleep
Around the dying embers of a fire,
It seemed
A symbol of their souls
That cling
To dead and dying things in search of warmth.

I crept away into the night
Alone
And closed my eyes - it was in vain,
I saw them still, I saw their eyes
Devoid of every light
But life itself

I thought of Him Who came
To give
Beauty for ashes,
The oil of joy for mourning, praise for grief:
But still they live
And die
Beneath the weight and burden of their fears.

I saw them as they are
It was enough
I think I never shall blot out the sight;
I did not hear them speak
But ever since
I hear within my heart
Their ceaseless crying.

Forgetting what lies behind...

I feel it deep within, the ache
of sad things past that tore my heart
but deeper still the Spirit moves,
He bids me take another step,
while bright ahead His future gleams
with sweeter light it dares to gleam
and so I dare to hope ...

I cannot wipe away the past
nor stifle quite its sad refrain,
but life moves on with vigour swift
and I must move,
nor stop to take
a backward look with sighs and tears,
what might have been must with the years
give place to Jesus now ...

Joined in Heart

Life is full of small divides,
separating friend from friend,
sometimes we lose touch awhile
as our pathways twist and bend;
Time and distance intervene,
just as streams divide their shores,
till an ocean lies between
some who shared their way before.
– Still, such waters may be crossed,
thoughts, like boats, may travel far,
taking us in mind and heart
where our friends and loved ones are;

since our thoughts are free as they,
friends are never far away.

iv. Family Services

Follow that Star

Come on, wise men,
now saddle your camels
and prepare for a journey
for you'll have to go far,
say goodbye to your wives, blow a kiss to the kiddies,
and get out on the highway and
follow that star!

There are shepherds abiding
in the fields on a hillside,
they are quietly guarding
their sheepish flock;
now the night sky is peaceful, and the shepherds are sleepy,
but they're about to be in for
a heaven of a shock!

Now the star is moving
and its wanting to guide you,
it will lead you to a stable
where angels are,
there's a baby in a manger
and He's going to be your Saviour,
so, come on, everybody, let's
Follow that star!

Gideon

Gideon was a weak little man
And Gideon led a poor little band
but Gideon was the best in the land
for the Lord said so

Gideon alone would have shivered in his shoes
but Gideon with God just couldn't lose
So Gideon said 'wherever you choose,
Then Lord I'll go'

So the Lord said to Gideon 'Now shake off your pallor
And go to Midian You mighty man of valour
For I will give them into your hand
And you shall deliver my people's land!'

So up leapt Gideon and gathered his band
And crept up on Midian as God had planned,
With a shout for the Lord and a light in his hand
Great Gideon and his mighty band
They saved old Israel's troubled land
For the Lord said so

Elijah and the Widow

– a rap for two or more people

There lived a king in days of old
His name was Ahab – and I'm told
He didn't have a heart of gold ...

In fact, he was an evil king
Who thought of every nasty thing
To keep his people suffering ...

His wife was even beastlier
But I decline to cause a stir
By spilling all the beans on her ...

Now one day God had had enough
Of all this rotten sinful stuff
'OK' he said, 'Now I'll get tough ...!'

God sent his prophet to the king
Elijah's message held a sting
A word of judgement he would bring ...

'Because you are a rotten bunch
God says it's coming to the crunch
– You won't be getting any lunch!

'There simply won't be any rain
To make your wheat grow lots of grain,
So – no more food! Till you think again!'

The king he didn't care at all,
He thought Elijah up the wall,
Until the rain refused to fall ...

It gave him quite a bad surprise
So 'lijah thought it might be wise
To hide himself from Ahab's eyes ...

The prophet found a handy cave
Beside a stream where he could laze
And while away the lonely days ...

There wasn't any food to hand
Because a famine hit the land,
But God had got it fully planned ...

He taught a flock of birds the trick
Of treating 'lijah like their chick
His food was fed him, beak to cheek

Then when the stream at last ran dry
Elijah said, 'Now I must fly,
So, all my feathered friends, goodbye!'

God led him next to Sidon's land,
To Zarephath where He had planned
To feed him by a widow's hand

This widow was a sorry dame,
She hadn't 10p to her name,
But she was friendly just the same ...

She was about to bake some bread
'It's all we have, my son,' she said
'When this is gone, we'll soon be dead' ...

'Share it with me!' The prophet cried,
'And you will find you're well supplied
With all your needs to keep alive' ...

The widow said, 'Don't think me rude,
But if I'm giving you our food,
I'm trusting God to make it good!' …

She did what 'lijah asked, all right
She fed him, and to her delight
God proved to her his power and might …

Her flour and oil did not run out,
God kept his word without a doubt,
And kept them going through the drought …

She hadn't much to serve Him with,
But God made sure that she would live
Because He moved her heart to give …

Though God was judging Ahab's greed
He still could see the widow's need,
To keep her fed was chicken-feed!

Baptism Rap

Jonah was a dude in the days of old
He was just a guy who wouldn't do what he was told
He tried to run away from God and jumped upon a ship
He said, 'Get me away from Him mighty quick!'
So the Lord sent a storm and the ship began to sink
And the sailors said, 'It really makes you think'
They said, 'Come on Jonah, pray like you oughta!'
Jonah said, 'Fellers, just throw me in the water!
Throw me in the water and the storm will calm
Throw me in the water and we'll all be safe from harm!'

I'll tell you now about another man
An army commander called Naaman
He thought he was special as the knees of a bee
Till one day he found he had leprosy!
'Help', he cried, 'What hope for me?
No-one wants to know you if you're HIV (or have leprosy)
Please God help!' Now Elisha heard his cry
And said 'Get in the water man before you die!
Get in the water and be thoroughly immersed
If you want to be rid of that terrible curse'
So he went right under and he came up clean
Like the sweetest new-born baby you've ever seen!

Now the gospels tell us of a guy called John
He was quite a weird cookie to look upon
But he knew what he was saying when he cried 'Repent!
Get into the water and declare your intent
To be dead to sin and alive to the Lord
You can be clean through the water and the word ...'
And the people listened and they flocked to the river
And prepared their hearts for the coming life-giver
That's Jesus!

Wonderful Spring!

A snowdrop uncurled from its slumber one day,
and said to the sun 'You're up early today!'
'Why yes', beamed the sun, 'because Spring's on the way!'

A crocus looked up from her warm, cosy bed
and gazed around slowly, then nodded her head,
'It seems to be time to get up now', she said

A little bud peeped from the branch of a tree,
and said 'something wonderful's happening to me,
and I'm just as sticky as sticky can be!'

A rustling began in the trunk of an oak,
and out popped a squirrel, who yawned as he spoke,
'My food is all gone, guess it's time I awoke!'

The spell of the winter which held earth so long,
is breaking, for earth has a spirit too strong,
and now she is waking to colour and song …

But as the world wakes, she is waiting to hear
the sound that announces the dawn of the year,
the herald that rings from the woods, loud and clear,
'Cuckoo! Cuckoo! Cuckoo! Spring is here!'

Section 2
Pastoral Poems

i. Infant Dedications

Joanna Stephanie

Secretly formed in the depths of the earth,
shaped by the heat and the fire,
chiselled and hammered in bringing to birth
beauty that all will admire ...
Polished and cut by a workman's hand,
lovingly weighed and refined,
all this to bring forth a gem for His crown,
fit for the place he designed ...

Joanna Stephanie, gift of the Lord,
purposed and planned for His love,
now may His Spirit like some holy sword
touch you with power from above ...
Give you authority, wisdom and grace,
joy, that will make the world sing,
forging your heart till it shines like a jewel
set on the brow of your King ...

For Samuel

Flame of Life
burn in this child
that by your energising power
he may grow strong in body, soul and mind,
that those in whom the flame is low
the spirit's candle flickering,
may take fresh oil from his free flow
and strength to live may find ...

Flame of Love
burn in this child
that gloriously, your cheering glow
may melt and warm the hurt, the hard, the cold ...
that in your purity of love
transcending every barrier
he may reveal throughout his life
a heart that grows not old ...

For Stephen Joel

A child should walk securely, unafraid
with sunshine ever round him
and an easy path to tread,
but this all fled
with that first catastrophic turning
from the light,
the loving paradise of Eden's God

Now stones and briars catch our feet,
the storm-clouds gather overhead,
at every turn the foe we meet
and we are called to be warriors instead ...

But Stephen, may you fight a worthy fight
and may you ever triumph in His might!

The world is full of semi-finished plans,
the tasks begun that fall beside the way,
the half-kept promises that let friends down,
the dreams that vanish in the light of day ...

But Stephen as you start your course today
May you run the race with Jesus all the way!

For Joel

Dear Dove of God, come near this child
that he may learn to recognise
the stirring of your wings
that he may know the mighty wind –
dividing oceans with its breath
now riffling gently through the down
to give a child sweet rest

Dear Dove of God stay near this child
that he may daily powerful grow
in partnership with you
and through your gentleness be strong
to touch the world's deep suffering
and by your overshadowing
loose healing from your wings...

For Kezia

Kezia
        We bind to you today a faithful heart
        A heart that loves and trusts the living word
A heart that beats in concert with your Lord
For He is called the Faithful One and True

We bind to you today a loyal heart
A heart that wills no evil to its friend
A heart whose love is constant to the end
As Jesus is to you

        Kezia, we bind you gladly to that love
Whose wisdom will instruct your inmost heart
We clothe you with His wisdom from the start
This is our gift to you …

For Olivia

Olivia Hope, God's honey-child,
we pray for you today
that you will draw the honey
from the rocks along life's way ...

That when the lion roars
(and the fearful stay indoors)
you may go to face him, singing, unafraid
not with sword of human greatness
but with songs of utter sweetness
you will quell his wrath and see his power fade ...

From the one who would devour you
will come strength that will empower you,
from the eater comes the honey you will eat ...
From the strong comes something sweet,
every problem that you meet
will become like ashes underneath your feet ...

Nothing evil will prevail
grace and love will never fail
as you trust His Spirit's overcoming might,
You will sing along life's way
when you hear the Spirit say
'Eat the honey, child, and let your eyes be bright ...'

For Edryd

We lifted you to heaven
on your Dedication day,
as the winter sun shone fondly on your head
through the multi-coloured windows
laughing sunbeams found their way
dancing lightly where the angels love to tread …

Oh your eyes were wide and watchful
and submissive as a saint's,
as we named the King of glory over you,
may He ever walk beside you,
may He be your guiding Star,
may He be to you the spring-rain and the dew …

May your life display His glory
as the light that shines within
shows the many-coloured wisdom of His mind,
may we read your inner story,
for the One who holds the key
opens up the treasure chest for us to find …

Oh precious child, you gave to us
the faith and power to pray,
– you were the perfect gift
that Christmas Day!

For Stephen John

Stephen John serenely sleeping,
Take your rest,
Let your mother safely fold you
To her breast;
You are blind to future choices which could lead your feet astray,
You are deaf to all the voices that would bid you go their way,
In your innocent simplicity we pray,
May you early prove 'His way is best.'

When you face those daily choices that will shape your future years,
When the voices that deceive are ringing loudly in your ears,
May you quickly learn to choose that better part;
No great evil will befall you
If you early hear Him call you,
'My son, give Me your heart.'

For Esther and Olivia

Children of Promise

Late in deciding to enter the world,
Yet coming with hope for the earth,
Children of promise, the heralds of spring,
Hearts cannot measure the joy that you bring,
Kairos – the time of your birth,
Whispering 'Father is never too late,
watch for the dawn of His word;
though He may tarry awhile, do not fear,
you are His children, so loved and so dear,
Enter the joy of your Lord!'

ii. Death & Loss

For Andrew
(a fine young man who died of cancer, aged 21 years)

Like the ark you tossed
upon turbulent seas
after weeks of rain,
your body still clinging to mountains of water
now lifted to heaven,
now hurled to the depths of your pain ...

Until hope, like a dove
came winging and singing
its way to your heart,
borne aloft on the wind of our prayers
and there in its mouth
so green and so new
(like your youth, like the dew)
a branch, a sweet promise of land ...

– A land where men walk free
and fires are built, and altars
to the One who guides them there in every weather,
and you smiled your enigmatic smile
and bade goodbye to seasickness forever ...

You made it safely to land, Andrew
not as a drifting wreck but a determined craft,
holding your branch of promise to the last ...
You grew so large inside
that life of every kind increased within you,
and you never let go of the dove
till He
and you
now safe ashore
could both go free

So tread the unknown shores with joy, dear Andrew
and pray that we who come behind
may also find
the shelter of that harbour
in our time ...

For Justin

(a precious baby who died when labour started prematurely)

Your heartbeat gave us hope that you
Would live to bless our lives
To fill your home and universe
With childhood's glad surprise
And through the days of struggle
When the waters broke our hearts
You kept alive the fire of faith
And helped us play our part

You challenged us to love, to pray
To stand together now
To hold each other's hands and speak
The words of life and power
And when the heartache ended
And your strength began to fail
Our hopes rose up to heaven with you
And passed within the veil

And Justin, though we sorrow
That we will not know you here
We know that you are safe beyond
The grip of pain or fear
Your life was just too precious
To be squandered here on earth
The treasure's now in heaven
Where you've found your truest worth

For Deborah
(who died at birth)

A life too brief
to give you pain
but not too brief
for joy …
the bond of love grew strongly through the weeks …
she knew the joy of well-loved voices
speaking, singing, praying,
and learned to listen well, if not to speak …

Now she will hear, with that so well-tuned hearing,
the voice that calls forth sleepers from the grave
to live again …
and she will find returning to her strongly
the love and joy that she so freely gave …

For Trevor

(a fine musician, husband, father and friend who died
suddenly and unexpectedly)

Closer to the kingdom than we dreamed
(you took us all by surprise)
you yet held back from its glory here
– reluctant to step into the limelight
or afraid, perhaps, of showing imperfection
in the presence of the only perfect One …
cautiously you skirted
the edges of His kingdom
and followed Him from afar …

Yet there were moments when
the divine glory rested upon you,
and you
caught unexpectedly in its spotlight
reflected the radiance with open face
alight with joy
delighting in its warmth …
then hastily stepped back into the shadows
to hide behind the shutters of your fear …

Now there are no shutters, no veil,
nothing to hide that glory from you
nor you from that glory,
the One you dimly saw is now made known …

Bask in His sunshine, Trevor.
Be happy, be blessed,
in the presence of the One who has always loved you,
always watched over you,
drawing you gently to Himself
inch by reluctant inch …
Let yourself go there
as you never could here,
and delight in the love and forgiveness of
your eternal friend …

iii. Relationships

The Homecoming

Welcome home, dear daughter
welcome home!
your father has been watching at the gate ...
so come on in and dry your clothes and dry your eyes
it really doesn't matter that you're late ...

We've thought of you each moment of your journey
and many nights we've waited up for you
we pictured all the dark and lonely pathways
and prayed against all hope you'd make it through

And now you're here, and you're so welcome, dear
come by the fire and warm yourself awhile
tomorrow there'll be feasting, dancing, singing
tonight it is enough to see you smile

We will not speak of all that lies behind us
this is no time to dwell upon the past
our gentle tears are all that shall remind us
that dear one, you are truly home at last ...

Days of Pain (for JB)

I thought I could not face the days of pain
alone again –
it seemed too much for any mortal crumbling
frame to bear
but He knew better
and in my lonely valley of despair
when even life itself became a fetter
I found Him there ...
He did not come to me in robes of light
or joy too bitter-sweet
but in my sorrow's night
when down a dark and slippery path I trod
I felt a rock beneath my feet
and knew that it was God ...

Love's Paradox

Love is a mystery, hid in eternity
yet we may find its reflection on earth,
hints of the depth that's contained in its fullness
showing mere mortals where love has its birth.

Love in its essence is childishly simple
yet in expression how wonderfully wise!
hoping, believing, enduring the 'all things'
seeing the truths that are hid from our eyes.

Love is a paradox, growing in weakness
yet from that weakness deriving its strength,
thriving on obstacles, failures and heart-aches,
knowing no boundary, limit or length.

Yet love is humble, refusing to vaunt itself
turning its face from its own sacrifice
seeking no honour or praise for its service
love is like Jesus, and loving is Christ.

Summer

(To John and Sarah on their wedding)

'In Spring', they say, 'a young man's fancy
lightly turns to thoughts of love …'
– but is it only ever in the Spring?

There is a fruitful season
during summer's heady days
or the early autumn haze
when the trees begin a stirring deep within …

Long before they lose their glory
Or the leaves begin to fall
they produce amazing, blazing colour-bursts,
and in that crazy leafing lies the fullest glow of life
as the trees reach out to warm the cooling earth …

We are frazzled, razzled, dazzled
by their leaping dance of life,
the kaleidoscopic colours of their prime!
But the secret of this flourishing lies hidden, hidden deep,
where the trees know well their chosen glory-time …

Oh the Spring is full of fragile buds
and gentle shades of green,
and it brings a hopeful tear to watching eyes …
But the summer's full of ripened fruit
and shouts of startled joy,
and the laughter rises, rises to the skies! …

To our 'Baghdad Bag-Carrier'!

That we, when we so briefly met,
not having seen your face before
should know at once you were our friend, our brother,
This is the joy ...
– a look, a smile, a passing word,
some inner warmth exchanged and known,
and we were one
– one in the secret life which fires
our inmost soul,
one in the love of Him who died
to make us whole ...
All this we knew
instinctively
when first we met,
and from that day
though far apart
and out of touch
our paths may be,
It's strangely true,
we carry you
about with us
within our hearts ...

Section 3

Praise Poems

i. Praise & Worship

God so loved...

People living
      laughing
            crying
every breath a death denying
rise to greet the hopeful heartbeat
of their lives ...

People giving
      sharing
            daring
love's relentless sense still caring
dare to share the very air
where hope may thrive ...

Love forgiving
      staring
            bearing,
sin's polluted garment wearing
calling 'sheep, here is your shepherd,
come, and live ...!'

Praise Be!

Praise be to God for all earth's lovely things
– clear skies, still water, meadow, tree and flower,
beauty which lies about us every hour,
joy in the throat of every bird that sings;

surrounded by such loveliness,
such effortless tranquillity
as here we see,
we dare believe
that He who gives the earth its dress
will for His children do no less,
but clothe with love and joy and peace
all those who will receive.

The Hills

The rugged hills have ever stood
a witness to endurability;
'Some things', they seem to say, 'will never fall,
but stand in triumph over all,
unalterably good',
– such things as love and hope and trust,
friendship, and all things true and just,
– these things will prove to be
enduring, when all else is dust,
true tokens of a deeper immortality.

Surrounded

Hills surround Jerusalem,
Silent, watchful sentinels
against the foe
And God, like them, surrounds the trusting heart
with steadfast love, which wards off hell's assailing dart.
That this is so,
Praise God, the very weakest soul may know …

The Wild

The wild is very beautiful – rock, stone and tree,
bare hills, swift rivers, gorse and moss and fern,
– who would not gaze in awe at such stern majesty,
filled with exhilaration? – but we turn
homeward to quiet hearth and easy chair,
closing the door on all the wild world's calls,
happy to dwell within four solid walls,
content because one dear, loved face is there.

Serenity

Tell me not we're growing old
with every passing year;
No, tell me rather we are going on
from strength to strength,
reaching for some higher sphere,
until at length
we find we have acquired an inner quality,
a peace of heart and mind and soul,
– serenity,
a mind made whole,

a heart at one with nature, man and God.

Because...

(Inspired by Amy Carmichael's poem *Come, Lord Jesus*)

Because of earth's unending strife,
the wars that eat up human life
Because of hatred, race for race,
the fear of any different face
Because of children, hungry, cold
while men are heaping up their gold
Because the world has need of light
to end this long and painful night

We make our foremost prayer this day
'Your kingdom come, O Christ we pray' ...